You Can't Dance to These Rhythms

What Are Algorithms?

by Brian P. Cleary

illustrations by Martin Goneau

Millbrook Press • Minneapolis

An **algorithm** is a list of step-by-step instructions that solves a problem or completes a task,

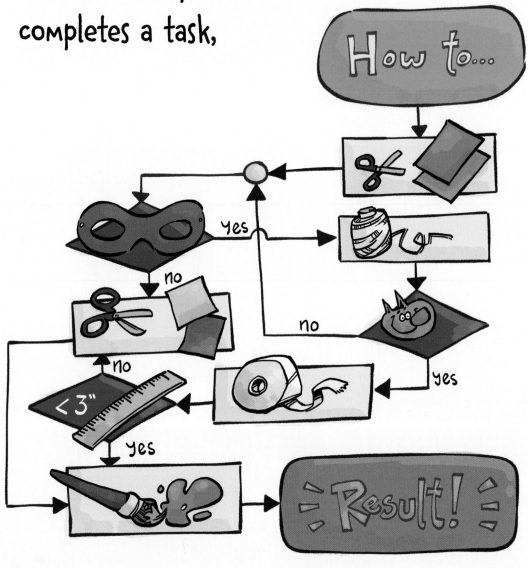

like what to do with scissors, markers, cardboard, string, and tape

to make yourself a truly awesome mask.

Recipes are algorithms, since
they walk you through

the steps to make a pizza or a cake.

They help explain procedure—all the whats and hows and whens,

ingredients, and how long things should bake.

The order of instructions in
an algorithm must
be followed perfectly for
its success.

When making chocolate cake, you
don't add eggs and salt and sugar
after it's been baked,
'cause that's a mess!

When it comes to coding,
an algorithm uses

a language such as C++ or Alice

to tell devices, step-by-step,
exactly what to do—
whether you're in Timbuktu or Dallas.

These tasks or problems have to be
chopped down to simple steps,
and algorithms help to lead the way

by making tasks much smaller—
more specific—so they're helpful
in solving little jobs throughout your day.

Take the task of feeding Kitty:
How do you do that?
"Feed the cat," does not give
us a plan.

Algorithm to Feed Kitty

1. Locate Kitty's food bowl.
2. Place bowl on counter.
3. Locate can of cat food.
4. Locate can opener.
5. Use can opener to remove lid from can.
6. Scoop contents from can into Kitty's bowl.
7. Recycle can.
8. Locate water bowl.
9. Run tap water into bowl until 3/4 full.
10. Place both bowls on Kitty's mat.

But take a look at all the details in our algorithm, and then you might begin to understand.

A computer without algorithms
wouldn't do a thing!
It couldn't play a movie,
song, or game.

It couldn't even add up
simple sums, like 2 + 2,
or help you check the spelling of a name.

A lot of algorithms even know how to adapt without a human making a decision.

Self-driving cars won't simply
go as fast as they can go—

their speed will change
according to conditions.

The algorithm's written so
depending on events,
the computer can respond a
certain way,

like if someone's detected in the crosswalk we're approaching, the car will stop until they've walked away.

Who can write an algorithm?
You can when you learn.
Then you'll tell your computer what to do.

Create a game? Or build a site?
Make an awesome app?
All it takes are coding skills—and you!

Do you know?

Coding is fun! And best of all, anyone can do it! All you need is a computer or tablet, an internet connection, and a willingness to try.

As you read in this book, algorithms are step-by-step instructions that tell a computer what to do. These instructions need to be small and simple so that the computer knows exactly what to do during each part of the process. Algorithms are used to do things that are as easy as adding numbers or as complicated as driving a car.

Here are some other things algorithms can do:

- play chess
- run a video game
- search the internet
- control a traffic light
- suggest another movie to watch
- find the fastest way from your house to a friend's house

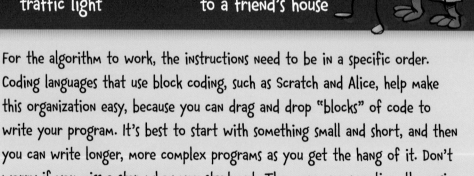

For the algorithm to work, the instructions need to be in a specific order. Coding languages that use block coding, such as Scratch and Alice, help make this organization easy, because you can drag and drop "blocks" of code to write your program. It's best to start with something small and short, and then you can write longer, more complex programs as you get the hang of it. Don't worry if you miss a step when you start out. The more you practice, the easier it will be!

Check out these great resources!

Books

Funk, Josh. *How to Code a Sandcastle*. New York: Viking Books for Young Readers, 2018. Follow along as Pearl and her robot friend Pascal figure out how to build a sandcastle by using code. They break down the problem into small steps and use concepts including loops and sequences to achieve their goal.

Loya, Allyssa. *Algorithms with* Frozen. Minneapolis: Lerner Publications, 2019. How do computers know what to do? Do they have brains? Of course not! People write lines of code that tell a computer what to do. Several lines of code make up an algorithm. You can write algorithms too, with the help of your favorite *Frozen* characters.

Lyons, Heather. *Learn to Program*. Minneapolis: Lerner Publications, 2017. Programs are instructions that computers follow. Learn about different programming languages, coding rules and bugs, and how to solve problems. Once you know the basics, use the link in this book to go online and try out your new skills.

Websites and Apps

Code.org
https://code.org
This site has lots of resources for anyone who wants to start coding—including students and their teachers. Check out the "Projects" tab to see what other kids have done and to take a look at the code for these projects.

Scratch Jr.
https://www.scratchjr.org
This simple, block-based programming language was created especially for early elementary students who don't have any previous coding experience. It runs on both iPads and Android tablets.

Find activities, games, and more at
www.brianpcleary.com

ABOUT THE AUTHOR & THE ILLUSTRATOR

BRIAN P. CLEARY is the author of the best-selling Words Are CATegorical® series, as well as the Sounds Like Reading® series, the Poetry Adventures series, and several others. He is also the author of *Crunch and Crack, Oink and Whack! An Onomatopoeia Story* and *The Sun Played Hide-and-Seek: A Personification Story*. He lives in Cleveland, Ohio.

MARTIN GONEAU is the illustrator of many books, including quite a number in the Words Are CATegorical™ series. When he is not drawing, he enjoys playing video games and learning how to code. He lives in Trois-Rivières, Québec, with his lovely wife and his two sons.

Thank you to technical expert Michael Miller for reviewing the text and illustrations.

Text copyright © 2019 by Brian P. Cleary
Illustrations copyright © 2019 by Lerner Publishing Group, Inc.

Millbrook Press
A division of Lerner Publishing Group, Inc.
241 First Avenue North
Minneapolis, MN 55401 USA

For reading levels and more information, look up this title at www.lernerbooks.com.

Main body text set in Chauncy Decaf Medium 27/36. Typeface provided by the Chank Company.
The illustrations in this book were created in Adobe Photoshop using a Wacom Cintiq Pro 16.

Library of Congress Cataloging-in-Publication Data

Names: Cleary, Brian P., 1959- author. | Goneau, Martin, author.
Title: You can't dance to these rhythms : what are algorithms? / Brian P. Cleary, Martin Goneau.
Description: Minneapolis : Millbrook Press, [2019] | Audience: Age 5-9. | Audience: K to Grade 3.
Identifiers: LCCN 2018022638 (print) | LCCN 2018033543 (ebook) | ISBN 9781541543874 (eb pdf) |
   ISBN 9781541533080 (lb : alk. paper) | ISBN 9781541545595 (pb : alk. paper)
Subjects: LCSH: Computer algorithms—Juvenile literature. | Cats—Care—Juvenile literature.
Classification: LCC QA76.9.A43 (ebook) | LCC QA76.9.A43 C54 2019 (print) | DDC 005.1—dc23

LC record available at https://lccn.loc.gov/2018022638

Manufactured in the United States of America
1-44877-35727-9/18/2018